Key Stage 3 Shakespeare

Scene-specific preparation for the
2008 national test

Much Ado About Nothing

Contents

The story of *Much Ado About Nothing*

1 | Leonato, with his daughter Hero and niece Beatrice, wait to meet Don Pedro, Prince of Aragon, and his nobles. Beatrice makes comments at the expense of one of the expected noblemen – Benedick – with whom she has a war of wit.

2 | Don Pedro, Prince of Aragon, returns victorious from war, accompanied by Claudio and Benedick, both successful soldiers. The war was against Don Pedro's own brother, Don John.

3 | Benedick is notorious for his rude remarks about women. He makes fun of Claudio for falling in love with Hero. Don Pedro, by contrast, agrees to woo Hero on Claudio's behalf, and does so.

4 | Don John, brother of Don Pedro, hates himself and the world. He takes pleasure in the idea of causing trouble for Don Pedro's favourite, Claudio.

5 | Beatrice enjoys having fun at a masked ball by describing Benedick rudely, when (supposedly) neither knows who the other one is.

6 | Claudio has been feeling jealous of Don Pedro. However, having wooed Hero on behalf of Claudio, Don Pedro gains Leonato's consent and then hands over to Claudio his 'jewel' Hero. To occupy the time before the wedding, Don Pedro intends to 'bring Signior Benedick and Lady Beatrice into a mountain of affection.'

7 | Don John's servant Borachio suggests a way of ruining the marriage by making it appear that Hero is unfaithful. His lover, Margaret, will call to him from a window so that the watchers (Claudio and Don Pedro) will mistake her for Hero.

8 | Knowing that Benedick can overhear them, the Prince, Claudio and Leonato speak of Beatrice's love for Benedick. They convince him that she does indeed 'dote' on him.

9 Hero and her gentlewomen speak of Benedick's love for Beatrice, knowing that she can overhear them.

10 Don John persuades Claudio and Don Pedro to join him to witness what he claims will be Hero's betrayal.

11 Claudio shames Hero at the moment when he was to marry her, and does so with maximum cruelty.

12 Friar Francis suggests that they change attitudes and the atmosphere by putting out news that Hero has died. Meanwhile, the local watch, although they are figures of fun, accidentally overhear and arrest Don John's villains, Conrade and Borachio.

13 Benedick promises Beatrice that he will challenge Claudio to defend Hero's honour.

14 Don John's plot is exposed by his servants who have been arrested by the Watch under Constable Dogberry.

15 Thinking that Hero is dead, Claudio has agreed to marry Leonato's niece. He and Don Pedro go to what they think is Hero's tomb, only to find that the woman is Hero herself, back from the dead.

16 Beatrice and Benedick acknowledge their love for each other, but in their own witty ways and to the amusement of everyone.

Set extracts – *Much Ado About Nothing*

Extract 1: Act 4, Scene 1, lines 196 to 325

Language
The phrase 'pause awhile' indicates that this is a serious moment

Performance
The Friar should be positioned in the centre of the stage to show he is in charge at this point in the scene

Character
Leonato does not show much concern for how Hero is feeling; he is more concerned about his reputation

Performance
Leonato should pace back and forth across the stage to show how agitated he is

Language
The Friar's speech is in iambic pentameter and the steady rhythm acts to soothe Leonato and restore calm to the situation

Character
Claudio will grieve for Hero believing she has died. It is important that he feels this intensity of emotion, because that will make him willing to make amends for what he has done to her

Performance
Throughout the Friar's speech, Leonato should be walking about the stage, holding his head in hands to show that he feels defeated about what has happened

FRIAR
Pause awhile,
And let my counsel sway you in this case.
Your daughter here the Princes left for <u>dead</u>.
Let her awhile be secretly kept in,
And publish it that she is <u>dead</u> indeed.
Maintain a <u>mourning</u> ostentation;
And on your family's old monument
Hang <u>mournful epitaphs</u>, and do all rites
That appertain unto a <u>burial</u>.

LEONATO
What shall become of this? What will this do?

FRIAR
Marry, this, well carried, shall on her behalf
Change <u>slander to remorse</u>: that is some good.
But not for that dream I on this strange course,
But on this travail look for <u>greater birth</u>.
She dying, as it must be so maintained,
Upon the instant that she was accused,
Shall be lamented, pitied and excused
Of every hearer: for it so falls out
That what we have we prize not to the worth,
Whiles we enjoy it; but being lacked and lost
Why, then we rack the value, then we find
The virtue that possession would not show us
Whiles it was ours. So will it fare with Claudio.
When he shall hear <u>she died upon his words</u>,
Th' idea of her life shall sweetly creep
Into his study of imagination.
And every lovely organ of her life
Shall come apparelled in more precious habit,
More moving, delicate, and full of life,
Into the eye and prospect of his soul,
Than when she lived indeed. Then <u>shall he mourn</u>,
If ever love had interest in his liver,
And wish he had not so accused her –
<u>No, though he thought his accusation true</u>.
Let this be so, and doubt not but success
Will fashion the event in better shape
Than I can lay it down in likelihood.
But if all aim but this be levelled false.
The supposition of the lady's death
Will quench the wonder of her infamy.

Performance
Hero should be lying on the ground still unconscious. Beatrice should be kneeling over her, holding her hand, and weeping

Language
Repetition of the word 'dead' reflects the theme that Hero's reputation has been destroyed. The language of death and funerals adds to the seriousness of the situation

Language
Leonato's two short sentences are questions, which indicates how confused and upset he is by the situation

Theme
The Friar's plan offers Hero a chance to have her honour restored

Language
The word 'died' emphasises the horror of what Claudio has done – his words destroyed her happiness and reputation

Language
The Friar emphasises that Claudio, though in the wrong for his treatment of Hero, did it because he believed he was right. This prepares the audience and Leonato for accepting his plan to trick Claudio

Language
The phrase suggests re-birth or resurrection and is a sign of hope and a signal towards a happy ending

Performance
The Friar should lead Hero from the stage, his arm around her shoulders. Leonato follows behind them, his head hanging down, and walking in a way to show that he feels old and helpless

Character/ language
Benedick's formal address 'Lady Beatrice' is very important because in the past he has called her insulting names. It shows he now cares for her

Performance
Beatrice watches Hero leave the stage; she mops the tears from her eyes and shakes her head to show that she cannot believe what has happened to her

Language
The short sentences in this part of the scene contrast with the long sermon-like speech of the Friar. This is to inject pace into the exchange between Beatrice and Benedick and to show how agitated Beatrice is

Performance
Beatrice should walk quickly back and forth across the stage with Benedick following behind her. This shows she is distracted and is not interested in what he is saying to her

And if it sort not well, you may conceal her,
As best befits her <u>wounded reputation</u>,
In some reclusive and religious life,
Out of all eyes, tongues, minds and injuries.

BENEDICK
Signior Leonato, let the Friar advise you.
And though you know my inwardness and love
is very much unto the Prince and Claudio,
Yet, by <u>mine honour</u>, I will deal in this
As secretly and justly as your soul
Should with your body.

LEONATO
Being that I flow in grief,
The smallest twine may lead me.

FRIAR
'Tis well consented. Presently away:
For to strange sores strangely they strain the cure.
Come, lady, <u>die to live</u>. This wedding-day
Perhaps is but prolonged: have patience and endure.

All exit except Benedick *and* Beatrice.

BENEDICK
<u>Lady Beatrice</u>, have you wept all this while?

BEATRICE
Yea, and I will weep a while longer.

BENEDICK
I will not desire that.

BEATRICE
You have no reason: I do it freely.

BENEDICK
Surely I do believe your <u>fair cousin is wronged</u>.

BEATRICE
Ah, how much might the man deserve of me that
would <u>right her</u>!

BENEDICK
Is there any way to show such friendship?

Language
The word 'wounded' is normally used to describe soldiers hurt in battle. It emphasises how Hero has been cut by Claudio's savage accusation

Theme
Benedick is aware that his loyalty to his friends is now under considerable strain and that he will need to break these bonds if he is to support the Friar's plan. This shows that Benedick does not believe Claudio's accusation against Hero

Performance
The Friar should walk to where Hero is still lying on the ground, kneel down and with Beatrice's help raise her to her feet, symbolising that Hero has risen above Claudio's words and will be restored

Character
Benedick reveals his caring nature when he shows concern for Beatrice's distress. He is sensitive to her feelings and knows this is not the time for jokes. This gentle and supportive Benedick is very different from the one who used to ridicule Beatrice

Language
The use of 'fair' and 'wronged' stresses that Benedick does not believe Claudio's accusation

Theme/character
Beatrice makes it clear that she wants to avenge Hero and have her honour restored

Character

Benedick confesses his love for Beatrice, perhaps because he feels he needs to show her that he is the 'man' to help her

Performance

Benedick should stop Beatrice pacing about the stage, and make her face him when he tells her he loves her. Making her stand still and look at him means she has to concentrate on his words

Performance

Benedick should catch her hands to stop her moving away from him to show he is determined to continue the conversation because he believes she does love him

Language

Benedick builds on Beatrice's image of him eating his sword by claiming he will make any man who says he does not love her, eat his sword

---

BEATRICE
A very even way, but no such friend.

BENEDICK
May a man do it?

BEATRICE
It is a man's office, but not yours.

BENEDICK
I do love nothing in the world so well as you. Is not that strange?

BEATRICE
As <u>strange</u> as the thing I know not. It were as possible for me to say I loved nothing so well as you. <u>But believe me not, and yet I lie not: I confess nothing, nor I deny nothing, I am sorry for my cousin.</u>

BENEDICK
By my sword, Beatrice, thou lovest me.

BEATRICE
Do not swear and eat it.

BENEDICK
I will swear by it that you love me; and I will make him eat it that says I love not you.

BEATRICE
Will you not eat your word?

BENEDICK
With no sauce that can be devised to it. I protest I love thee.

BEATRICE
Why then, God forgive me!

BENEDICK
What offence, <u>sweet Beatrice?</u>

BEATRICE
You have stayed me in a happy hour. I was about to protest I loved *you*.

Character

Beatrice makes it clear that she does not expect Benedick to avenge Hero

Performance

When she says this line Beatrice should break away from Benedick to show she does not want to continue this conversation

Language

Beatrice picks up on the word 'strange' used by Benedick in the previous line. It shows that he has caught her attention

Language/character

The use of punctuation to break up the sentence shows how confused Beatrice feels because of Benedick's confession that he loves her and her reaction to Hero's humiliation

Language

The word 'sweet' shows Benedick's affection for Beatrice

BENEDICK
And do it with all thy heart.

BEATRICE
I love you with so much of my heart that none is left to protest.

BENEDICK
Come, bid me do anything for thee.

BEATRICE
Kill Claudio.

BENEDICK
Ha! Not for the wide world.

BEATRICE
You kill me to deny it. Farewell.

BENEDICK
Tarry, sweet Beatrice.

BEATRICE
I am gone though I am here. There is no love in you. Nay, I pray you, let me go.

BENEDICK
Beatrice –

BEATRICE
In faith, I will go.

BENEDICK
We'll be friends first.

BEATRICE
You dare easier be friends with me than fight with mine enemy.

BENEDICK
Is Claudio thine enemy?

BEATRICE

Is he not approved in the height a villain that hath slandered, scorned, dishonoured my kinswoman? O that I were a man! What, bear her in hand until they come to take hands, and then, with public accusation, uncovered slander, unmitigated rancour – O God, that I were a man! I would eat his heart in the market-place.

BENEDICK

Hear me, Beatrice –

BEATRICE

Talk with a man out at a window! A proper saying!

BENEDICK

Nay, but Beatrice –

BEATRICE

Sweet Hero! She is wronged, she is slandered, she is undone.

BENEDICK

Beat –

BEATRICE

Princes and counties! Surely, a princely testimony, a goodly count, Count Comfect – a sweet gallant, surely! O that I were a man for his sake; or that I had any friend would be a man for my sake! But manhood is melted into curtsies, valour into compliment; and men are only turned into tongue, and trim ones, too. He is now as valiant as Hercules that only tells a lie and swears it. I cannot be a man with wishing: therefore I will die a woman with grieving.

BENEDICK

Tarry, good Beatrice. By this hand, I love thee.

BEATRICE

Use it for my love some other way than swearing by it.

BENEDICK

Think you in your soul the Count Claudio hath wronged Hero?

BEATRICE

Yea, as sure as I have a thought or a soul.

BENEDICK
Enough: I am engaged. I will challenge him. I will kiss your hand, and so I leave you. By this hand, Claudio shall render me a dear account. As you hear of me, so think of me. Go comfort your cousin: I must say she is dead; and so, farewell.

Exeunt.

Extract 2: Act 5, Scene 4

At Leonato's house.
Enter Leonato, Antonio, Benedick, Beatrice, Margaret, Ursula, Friar Francis *and* Hero.

FRIAR
Did I not tell you she was innocent?

LEONATO
So are the Prince and Claudio, who accused her
Upon the error that you heard debated.
But Margaret was in some fault for this,
Although against her will, as it appears
In the true course of all the question.

ANTONIO
Well, I am glad that all things sort so well.

BENEDICK
And so am I, being else by faith enforced
To call young Claudio to a reckoning for it.

LEONATO
Well, daughter, and you gentlewomen all,
Withdraw into a chamber by yourselves;
And when I send for you, come hither masked.
The Prince and Claudio promised by this hour
To visit me. You know your office, brother:
You must be father to your brother's daughter,
And give her to young Claudio.

Exit Hero, with Beatrice, Margaret *and* Ursula.

ANTONIO
Which I will do with confirmed countenance.

Language

The play on the words 'bind' and 'undo' indicate Benedick's inner turmoil about marriage. The word 'undo' has a double meaning – it could be freedom, but also can mean someone being ruined

Theme

The word 'eye' reflects a major theme of the play – that our eyes can deceive us, as in the case of Claudio with Hero, and can also blind us to our true feelings, as with Beatrice and Benedick

Language

Leonato picks up the theme of sight to remind Benedick that he was the one who gave him the information that enabled him to see Beatrice in a romantic way

Performance

Leonato should bow first to Don Pedro and then to Claudio. This shows that irrespective of what Claudio has done, Leonato has not forgotten his manners. By repeating 'good morrow' he is showing that all is well with this day

BENEDICK
Friar, I must entreat your pains, I think.

FRIAR
To do what, signior?

BENEDICK
To bind me, or undo me – one of them.
Signior Leonato, truth it is, good signior,
Your niece regards me with an eye of favour.

LEONATO
That eye my daughter lent her. 'Tis most true.

BENEDICK
And I do with an eye of love requite her.

LEONATO
The sight whereof I think you had from me,
From Claudio, and the Prince. But what's your will?

BENEDICK
Your answer, sir, is enigmatical.
But, for my will, my will is your good will
May stand with ours, this day to be conjoined
In the state of honourable marriage –
In which, good Friar, I shall desire your help.

LEONATO
My heart is with your liking.

FRIAR
And my help.
Here comes the Prince and Claudio.

Enter Don Pedro *and* Claudio *with attendants.*

DON PEDRO
Good morrow to this fair assembly.

LEONATO
Good morrow, Prince; good morrow, Claudio.
We here attend you. Are you yet determined
Today to marry with my brother's daughter?

Performance

Benedick should draw the Friar aside and bring him to the front of the stage. This shows the audience that this is an important moment because Benedick, the man who at the beginning of the play vowed he would never marry, is going to ask the Friar to officiate at his marriage to Beatrice

Theme/character

Benedick's description of marriage as 'honourable' is important – it shows how much he has changed his view of love and marriage. This is a far cry from claims in Act 1 that he will 'die a bachelor'

Language

Benedick's rambling speech – he takes a long time to get to the point – reflects how hard it is for him to confess in front of everyone that he wants to marry Beatrice

Language

The Prince's formal address reflects the change in the relationship. At the start of the play, Don Pedro was more informal and relaxed when addressing Leonato. He and his attendants should bow to Leonato to show their respect

Performance

Benedick should stand away from Don Pedro and Claudio to show that he is not part of their group any more. He should wait for Don Pedro to approach him to show that he has less respect for him now

Character

Claudio does not see that his sexual banter with Benedick is inappropriate – it is a sign that he is immature and insensitive

Performance

Benedick should face Claudio and look him straight in the eyes when he delivers these lines. He should speak in a cold, harsh tone to make it clear to Claudio that he is not joining in with his attempts to joke about sex

Theme/character

Benedick is insulting Claudio's honour by suggesting that his mother was unfaithful and he is not his father's son. The theme of infidelity in marriage was joked about in the opening scene; here it is meant to upset Claudio

Language

The use of the pronouns 'she' and 'her' stresses the impersonal arrangement of this wedding: the bride is not even given a name

---

CLAUDIO
I'll hold my mind, were she an Ethiope.

LEONATO
Call her forth, brother, here's the Friar ready.

Exit Antonio

DON PEDRO
Good morrow, Benedick. Why, what's the matter,
That you have such a February face,
So full of frost, of storm and cloudiness?

CLAUDIO
I think he thinks upon the savage bull.
Tush, fear not, man, we'll tip thy horns with gold,
And all Europa shall rejoice at thee,
As once Europa did at lusty Jove,
When he would play the noble beast in love.

BENEDICK
Bull Jove, sir, had an amiable low –
And some such strange bull leaped your father's cow,
And got a calf in that same noble feat
Much like to you, for you have just his bleat.

CLAUDIO
For this I owe you. Here comes other reckonings.

Enter Antonio, with Hero, Beatrice, Margaret and Ursula, wearing masks.

Which is the lady I must seize upon?

ANTONIO
This same is she, and I do give you her.

CLAUDIO

Why then, she's mine. Sweet, let me see your face.

LEONATO

No, that you shall not, till you take her hand
Before this Friar, and swear to marry her.

CLAUDIO
Give me your hand: before this holy Friar,
I am your husband, if you like of me.

Language/character

Claudio is sorry for what he said about Hero and what has happened to her. He is vowing to marry his new bride, even if he does not find her attractive

Language

The images of winter reflect the changed relationship between Benedick and Claudio and the Prince

Character

Claudio tries to re-establish his friendship with Benedick by making crude sexual jokes. It shows he has not fully understood how Benedick's respect and affection for him have changed

Language

The word 'bleat' is a sharp insult to Claudio. It suggests he is weak and immature

Language/theme

The word 'seize' reflects the theme that this marriage is not a romantic liaison, but a loveless affair. Claudio goes on to claim his new bride with the words 'she's mine'

Theme

Claudio is being deceived because he cannot 'see' his new bride's face

Performance

The unmasking is a key moment in the scene so Hero needs to command the stage. She should be standing in the same place as she did for the first wedding, with Claudio facing her. She should stress the words 'other wife' and 'other husband' to show Claudio she has forgiven him

Performance

When Hero removes her mask Claudio should step back in amazement, look at Don Pedro who is standing beside him, and then back at Hero. He should stress the word 'another' to show he is completely bewildered by what is happening

Language

Benedick repeats Beatrice's words to show that he knows she is joking with him

HERO (*Unmasking*)
And when I lived, I was your other wife;
And when you loved, you were my other husband.

CLAUDIO
Another Hero!

HERO
Nothing certainer.
One Hero died defiled, but I do live;
And surely as I live I am a maid.

DON PEDRO
The former Hero! Hero that is dead!

LEONATO
She died, my lord, but whiles her slander lived.

FRIAR
All this amazement can I qualify,
When, after that the holy rites are ended,
I'll tell you largely of fair Hero's death.
Meantime let wonder seem familiar,
And to the chapel let us presently.

BENEDICK
Soft and fair, Friar. Which is Beatrice?

BEATRICE (*Unmasking*)
I answer to that name. What is your will?

BENEDICK
Do not you love me?

BEATRICE
Why no – no more than reason.

BENEDICK
Why, then your uncle and the Prince and Claudio
Have been deceived. They swore you did.

BEATRICE
Do not you love me?

BENEDICK
Troth, no – no more than reason.

Language

The word 'other' signals that the deception is over and Hero has been reborn. The slur on her virtue has been washed away by her symbolic death

Performance

Hero should speak these lines in a confident voice to show that she has matured from this experience. She should stress the words 'I am a maid' to show Claudio that she knows he was wrong

Theme

Hero could not live in society while her reputation was in ruins. The words 'died' and 'lived' remind us of her re-birth or re-introduction to society

Character

Beatrice does not wait for the Friar to identify her. She steps forward to face Benedick. She should say the lines 'What is your will?' in an impatient voice to show that she is back to her old self. She and Benedick should be centre stage to show they are the important characters now

Language/character

Beatrice repeats the same question to Benedick to show that she can match him and is not going to let him outwit her. The question is almost a challenge

Theme

Many characters have been deceived in this play – the deception played on Beatrice and Benedick is about to be revealed

BEATRICE
Why, then my cousin, Margaret and Ursula
Are much deceived: for they did swear you did.

BENEDICK
They swore that you were almost sick for me.

BEATRICE
They swore that you were well-nigh dead for me.

Language

Beatrice has won this short battle of words. She tops Benedick's claim that she was sick with love for him, by using the words 'well-nigh dead' to show how desperate he was

Language

Beatrice and Benedick pick this word to show that they are playing around, but it also shows they are listening very carefully to one another

BENEDICK
'Tis no such matter. Then you do not love me?

BEATRICE
No truly, but in friendly recompense.

Language

Benedick knows she has won that round so changes tactics. The question is now phrased so that he shows he is not quite so sure that she does love him

Performance

Beatrice should turn away from Benedick when she says this, to show that he is going to have to try harder to get her to confess she loves him. She should stress the word 'friendly' to let him and everyone else know she is not going to say she loves him

LEONATO
Come, cousin, I am sure you love the gentleman.

CLAUDIO
And I'll be sworn upon't, that he loves her;
For here's a paper written in his hand,
A halting sonnet of his own pure brain,
Fashioned to Beatrice.

HERO
And here's another,
Writ in my cousin's hand, stolen from her pocket,
Containing her affection unto Benedick.

Theme

'Love' and 'affection' are necessary emotions for a happy marriage. The signs are very positive for Beatrice and Benedick

BENEDICK
A miracle! Here's our own hands against our hearts,
Come, I will have thee: but, by this light, I take thee for pity.

BEATRICE
I would not deny you; but, by this good day, I yield upon great persuasion – and partly to save your life, for I was told you were in a consumption.

Language

The use of the pronoun 'our' is a change from the use of 'I' and 'you' – it shows Benedick is sure she loves him and that they will become a married couple

Character

Now that the plot to deceive Claudio and restore Hero has been successful, Beatrice and Benedick relax back into their old verbal sparring. This is a good sign because we know that now they are doing it without intending to hurt one another

BENEDICK
Peace! I will stop your mouth. (*Kissing her*)

DON PEDRO
How dost thou, Benedick the married man?

Performance

When Benedick kisses Beatrice the other characters should applaud to show they approve of his actions. After he has kissed her, Beatrice should look happy and contented – his actions have ended their war of words and she does not speak again

Language

'Peace' is what Benedick will not have in his marriage to such a spirited and witty woman

Theme/character

This is a startling admission for Benedick the soldier to make. The view we have had of men in this play takes on another dimension – 'giddy' is a term used for fickle women. Here Benedick is saying men can be unreliable too

Theme

The word 'double-dealer' reminds us that this is what Claudio accused Hero of being. Claudio's view of marriage is not as honourable as Benedick's – he thinks Benedick will cheat on Beatrice if she does not keep an eye on him

Performance

Benedick is dictating what happens now. He should be standing in the centre of the stage, holding Beatrice's hand to show she is his. The rest of the cast should be behind when the music starts, he and Beatrice should be the first couple to start to dancing to show that they have become the centre of attention

BENEDICK
I'll tell thee what, Prince. A college of wit-crackers cannot flout me out of my humour. Dost thou think I care for a satire or an epigram? No: if a man will be beaten with brains, 'a shall wear nothing handsome about him. In brief, since I do purpose to marry, I will think nothing to any purpose that the world can say against it. And therefore never flout at me for what I have said against it – for man is a giddy thing, and this is my conclusion. For thy part, Claudio, I did think to have beaten thee: but in that thou art like to be my kinsman, live unbruised, and love my cousin.

CLAUDIO
I had well hoped, thou wouldst have denied Beatrice, that I might have cudgelled thee out of thy single life, to make thee a double-dealer – which out of question thou wilt be, if my cousin do not look exceeding narrowly to thee.

BENEDICK
Come, come, we are friends. Let's have a dance ere we are married, that we may lighten our own hearts and our wives' heels.

LEONATO
We'll have dancing afterward.

BENEDICK
First, of my word! Therefore play, music. Prince, thou art sad: get thee a wife, get thee a wife! There is no staff more reverend than one tipped with horn.

Enter a Messenger.

MESSENGER
My lord, your brother John is ta'en in flight,
And brought with armed men back to Messina.

BENEDICK
Think not on him till tomorrow. I'll devise thee brave punishments for him. Strike up, pipers!

Dance.

Exeunt.

Performance

Now that he has secured Beatrice Benedick is in a very confident mood. He should say this speech in a light-hearted, but still assertive way

Performance

Benedick should turn to Claudio and offer him his hand to show him that he is prepared to forget the past now that they will be part of the same family

Language

Benedick brings to an end Claudio's attempt to joke with him. The phrase 'come, come' makes it clear to Claudio that he has had enough of the same old jokes about sex

Language

The phrase 'our wives' shows that Benedick has adjusted quickly to the thought of being married

Language/character

The repetition of Benedick's advice to the Prince is a sign of how Benedick has changed since the start of the play, from the man who vowed never to marry, to one who wants all his friends to be married

Character response grid (PEEE)

Think about the statements in the first column, and fill in your response in the appropriate column, giving the evidence from the set extracts, then explaining and exploring your thinking. The first line has been completed for you as an example.

Statement	Response	Y/N	Evidence	Explanation	Exploration
The audience are more involved with Beatrice and Benedick than with Hero and Claudio	Definitely Yes, on balance Not really No way	Yes	*Bea: Kill Claudio.* *Ben: Enough: I am engaged. I will challenge him.* *Claudio: I am your husband, if you like of me.* *Don Pedro: Benedick the married man.*	Beatrice and Benedick say more and are centre stage. We are interested and entertained by their wit and their inevitable marriage. Hero is just the silent victim and deceived Claudio is a victim too.	Beatrice's passion is powerful, and has near-tragic intensity, whilst Benedick chooses love before loyalty to his friend. We care about their choices and their relationship. By contrast Hero and Claudio are more passive – they don't choose, they are just manipulated by others.
Claudio just doesn't deserve Hero as his wife	Definitely Yes, on balance Not really No way				
Beatrice and Benedick don't really love each other, even at the end of the play	Definitely Yes, on balance Not really No way				
Beatrice is a more appealing character than Benedick in these extracts	Definitely Yes, on balance Not really No way				
The Duke may have the power, but his impact on the audience in these extracts is insignificant	Definitely Yes, on balance Not really No way				
The interest for the audience is not whether Beatrice will marry Benedick, but how that comes to happen	Definitely Yes, on balance Not really No way				

Focus on character

Highlight the key words in the tables below and fill in the blank rows with your own points, quotations and personal responses.

Extract 1: Act 4, Scene 1, lines 196 to 325

Points	Quotations	Personal responses
Other characters The Friar is calm and reasonable, hence his solemn language, but Leonato is too distressed and bewildered to think or speak sensibly. Beatrice is weeping on stage.	Friar: publish it that she is dead indeed. Maintain a mourning ostentation; or Leonato: What shall become of this? What will this do? Leonato: … I flow in grief,	The audience know that Hero is innocent, but distraught Leonato and weeping Beatrice show us what damage has been done. Leonato's choice of the word 'flow' picks up Beatrice's tears.
Benedick His loyalty towards Claudio and the Prince is clear, but in spite of that he commits himself to Hero's cause, partly for Beatrice's sake.	Benedick: … my inwardness and love Is very much unto the Prince and Claudio, Yet, by mine honour, I will deal in this … secretly and justly …	Benedick comes through on stage as a man of emotion and integrity: his 'inwardness' shows that he cares about justice and honour as well as about Beatrice and her family.
Benedick is courteously concerned about Beatrice. At this time of heightened emotion he declares his love, although admitting that it is 'strange', given their past enmity.	Benedick: Lady Beatrice, have you wept all this while? Benedick: I do love nothing in the world so well as you. Is not that strange?	Benedick swings through a range of moods during this extract – supportive concern for Leonato; loving banter with Beatrice in which he declares his love.
He is shocked by Beatrice's 'Kill Claudio', but when convinced by her is prepared to challenge his former friend.	Benedick: Ha! Not for the wide world.	He is shocked at her venomous hatred for Claudio.
He is finally ready to be judged by his deeds and reputation – 'I am engaged'.	Benedick: Enough: I am engaged. I will challenge him. … As you hear of me, so think of me. Go comfort your cousin: I must say she is dead;	His initial shock is followed by a resolute determination to fight for her family's honour and to lie in a good cause.
Beatrice Beatrice's weeping on stage is a signal of how deeply she has been affected by Hero's humiliation.	Beatrice: It were as possible for me to say I loved nothing so well as you	Beatrice has been upset by her cousin's shame and confused by her own feelings towards Benedick. The uncertainty in their declarations of love comes through expressions full of negatives – 'not' and 'nothing' are used frequently.
In the midst of the banter about love her emotion breaks through.	Beatrice: I am sorry for my cousin	We see the depth of Beatrice's emotion here, signalled through her change in tone.
The fierce hatred of 'Kill Claudio' takes Benedick by surprise.	Beatrice: Kill Claudio. or Beatrice: There is no love in you.	The fierceness of 'Kill Claudio' changes the mood of the scene. Beatrice (not a conventionally helpless woman like Hero) now counts readiness to kill as the only acceptable sign of love.
She is conscious of her helplessness as a woman, but the violence of her thoughts and words could match those of any man.	Beatrice: O that I were a man! What, bear her in hand until they come to take hands,…. or O God, that I were a man! I would eat his heart in the market-place.	She, not Benedick, is the one taking the lead. Her words are violent, and she speaks like a man defending the family honour.
Beatrice, once 'My Lady Tongue', now shames Benedick into action.	Beatrice: … men are only turned into tongue,…. I cannot be a man with wishing: therefore I will die a woman with grieving.	Her words are formal and rhetorical and so persuasive that she convinces Benedick. Men have become mere 'tongues'.

Focus on character

Highlight the key words in the tables below and fill in the blank rows with your own points, quotations and personal responses.

Extract 2: Act 5, Scene 4

Points	Quotations	Personal responses
Other characters At the start of this extract Don Pedro says that Benedick looks gloomy: he may be pretending that he must still call Claudio to a 'reckoning' for his shaming of Hero, but he has not forgiven Claudio for what he did to Hero. He twists Claudio's animal image to insult him.	*Don Pedro: ...you have such a February face* *Benedick: ...got a calf in that same noble feat* *Much like to you, for you have just his bleat.*	The audience, like some of the characters, know the truth. The interest lies in how the characters who think Hero is dead will behave. Don Pedro's attempted jocularity is partly to disguise his discomfort at the situation he is how in. Jokes about adultery and sex no longer amuse Benedick because, to marry Beatrice, he must become less of a man's man and more of a lover.
Benedick Benedick's u-turn on marriage is meant to be funny, but there is an edge to his exchange with Claudio.	*Don Pedro: Benedick the married man?* *Benedick: ...to be conjoined* *In the state of honourable marriage –*	Because there is no longer any real tension over the evil deception of Claudio and Hero, the audience's interest is in what will happen over the loving deception of Beatrice and Benedick.
The 'not' is a clue to Benedick's uncertainty despite what he has been told of Beatrice's love for him. Like her he then claims to love 'no more than reason'.	*Beatrice: Do not you love me?* *Benedick: ...no more than reason.*	This echoing of each other's words indicates a unity of feeling beneath the surface of their war of wit.
Caught out by his own love poetry, he makes his move towards marriage and silences Beatrice with a kiss.	*Benedick: A miracle! Here's our own hands against our hearts.* *Come, I will have thee: but, by this light, I take thee for pity.* *Benedick: Peace! I will stop your mouth. (Kissing her)*	After their 'merry war' of noisy words throughout the play, their love is shown in a silent kiss. The audience will get the joke: only love can silence Beatrice.
Benedick knows that his change of view on marriage leaves him open to ridicule, and laughs at himself before others can laugh at him.	*Benedick: ... since I do purpose to marry, I will think nothing to any purpose that the world can say against it. And therefore never flout at me for what I have said against it – for man is a giddy thing, and this is my conclusion.* **or** *Benedick: ... Prince, thou art sad: get thee a wife, get thee a wife!*	Far from being humiliated, Benedick takes control in the final scene – he is the one who postpones dealing with Don John, and he swings the mirthful attention from himself to the Prince.
Beatrice Beatrice goes back to teasing and playing games as soon as Hero is safe.	*Beatrice: ...no more than reason.*	Although still witty, Beatrice is not quite 'My Lady Disdain' of earlier in the play.
Beatrice's exchanges with Benedick remind us that both have been deceived into declarations of affection. Both consent to loving for the sake of the other.	*Beatrice: Why, then my cousin, Margaret and Ursula* *Are much deceived: for they did swear you did.* *Beatrice: ...I yield upon great persuasion – and partly to save your life.....*	By now we know that she and Benedick deserve each other in a positive way. Significantly, she says nothing after being silenced with a kiss. The audience could interpret this in very different ways.

Focus on theme

Mark brief quotations in your extracts using a different coloured highlighter for each of the themes shown below. Add your own quotations and annotations for these and for other themes you think are important.

Deception

Points	Quotations	Personal responses
Extract 1 The Friar uses deception to bring out the truth and refute the false accusations against Hero that were based on Don John's deception.	*Friar: …publish it that she is dead indeed…* **or** *Come, lady, die to live.*	There is often a gap between appearance and reality: images of sight and eyes are frequent. Events on stage are not real, but can bring out truths.
Beatrice was never deceived about Hero – she has the insight of real affection and knows that the accusations are false. Beatrice is convinced by what she believes, not by what she sees.	*Beatrice: Talk with a man out at a window!…* *Sweet Hero! She is wronged, she is slandered, she is undone.* *Benedick: Think you in your soul the Count Claudio hath wronged Hero?* *Beatrice: Yea, as sure as I have a thought or a soul.*	Beatrice has depth as a character (that's why we care about her) and does not judge on superficial evidence like Claudio and the Prince. This makes her worthy of Benedick's love and the audience's admiration.
Extract 2 Seeing that the Prince and Claudio were deceived, Leonato joins in the new deception.	*Leonato: …the Prince and Claudio, who accused her* *Upon the error that you heard debated.*	This is not a tragedy, but Leonato's forgiveness does seem rather hasty.
Claudio, as before, wants to rely on what he can see, but that will no longer do, as he realises.	*Claudio: …Sweet, let me see your face.* *Leonato: No, that you shall not, till you take her hand…* *Claudio: I am your husband, if you like of me.*	Claudio is a shallow character who needed to learn not to judge on superficial evidence such as beauty or apparent betrayal.
Deception, which brought such suffering to Hero, here brings happiness to Beatrice and Benedick.	*Benedick: Why, then your uncle and the Prince and Claudio* *Have been deceived. They swore you did.* *Beatrice: Why, then my cousin, Margaret and Ursula* *Are much deceived: for they did swear you did.*	Appearances are deceptive throughout the play, and bring horror or (as here) happiness to the four main characters.

Honour and revenge

Points	Quotations	Personal responses
Extract 1 What happened had tragic potential: family honour was outraged and a daughter's life endangered, hence Leonato's distress. Even if the Friar's plan is not successful, it will help to save the family honour and protect Hero.	*… on your family's old monument* *Hang mournful epitaphs* *Leonato: What shall become of this? What will this do?* *Friar: … The supposition of the lady's death* *Will quench the wonder of her infamy.* *…you may conceal her,* *As best befits her wounded reputation…*	This is about public family honour as well as private personal suffering. Appearances count in this play.
Despite his friendship with Claudio and the Prince, Benedick sides with Beatrice.	*Benedick: Enough: I am engaged. I will challenge him.* *Benedick: As you hear of me, so think of me.*	Honour is a key theme. Benedick is an honourable soldier and uses the language of honour: *engaged.*
Beatrice sees the test of Benedick's love as being ready to kill his friend who has dishonoured her family.	*Beatrice: Kill Claudio.* *… a villain that hath slandered, scorned, dishonoured my kinswoman* *Sweet Hero! She is wronged, she is slandered, she is undone.*	There is depth of feeling here from both characters. The command to kill is a shock, but then Beatrice's sense of her family's dishonour becomes clear.
Extract 2 Benedick was ready to fight Claudio for Hero's honour, but is relieved now.	*Benedick: … being else by faith enforced* *To call young Claudio to a reckoning for it.*	The code of honour has been questioned and used as grounds for cruelty, but the mood has changed.
Claudio now wishes to rescue his honour by marrying someone he has not seen.	*Claudio: Which is the lady I must seize upon?*	Claudio is still using a soldier's violent language in the battle to restore his honour.
Benedick acknowledges that the time for revenge is past and	*Benedick: For thy part, Claudio, I did think to have beaten thee: but in*	The focus has moved from honour and revenge to the marriages, but this

Focus on theme

Mark brief quotations in your extracts using a different coloured highlighter for each of the themes shown below. Add your own quotations and annotations for these and for other themes you think are important.

Love and marriage

Points	Quotations	Personal responses
Extract 1 The Friar reminds us how badly Claudio has treated Hero. Claudio loves because of what he sees, and hates because of what he thinks he sees.	*Friar: When he shall hear she died upon his words, / Th' idea of her life shall sweetly creep / Into his study of imagination.*	It was a strange love that depended on the appearance of beauty and then of misconduct, and could turn so quickly to hate.
At this time of high emotion Benedick and Beatrice finally declare their love, but in a way that continues their 'merry war' of words.	*Benedick: I do love nothing in the world so well as you. Is not that strange? Beatrice: ...It were as possible for me to say I loved nothing so well as you.*	Negative expressions of positive feelings – *nothing, not* – but they do mean something, whereas Claudio's conventional declarations of love meant nothing.
Benedick makes joking references to war to prove his love, but Beatrice is serious in saying that only killing can prove Benedick's love for her.	*Benedick: By my sword, Beatrice, thou lovest me. ...Come, bid me do anything for thee. Beatrice: Kill Claudio. ...There is no love in you.*	*Kill Claudio* shocks Benedick, and the audience, since the recent talk has been about love. Love is linked with death as at the start of the extract, but in a different way.
Extract 2 Benedick sounds almost like a priest when he talks of marriage, not at all like his earlier self.	*Benedick: ...this day to be conjoined / In the state of honourable marriage –*	Benedick is a source of laughter because he is so changed from his determination to die single.
Benedick has been trying to silence Beatrice from the start. At last she is silenced with a kiss.	*Benedick: Peace! I will stop your mouth. (Kissing her)*	Language has limitations for everyone, not just for Dogberry. Actions here speak louder than words.
This is an echo of what was said earlier, and what Benedick said would never happen. Once its fiercest critic, he now recommends marriage.	*Don Pedro: How dost thou, Benedick the married man? Benedick: Prince, thou art sad: get thee a wife, get thee a wife!*	This is the line the audience have been waiting for. Don John's conspiracy is almost ignored in the celebrations.

Men and women

Points	Quotations	Personal responses
Extract 1 For a woman of noble birth, loss of reputation means loss of everything. Her disgrace affects her whole family.	*Friar: When he shall hear she died upon his words... ...This wedding-day Perhaps is but prolonged: have patience and endure.*	The public world of war and power is dominated by men, not by women.
Beatrice's language is as fierce and violent as a man's, but she knows she needs a man to fight for her. At this point her desire is for revenge rather than justice. She knows that Benedick cares about his honour and shames him into responding on behalf of Hero.	*Beatrice: Ah, how much might the man deserve of me that would right her!* **or** *... It is a man's office, but not yours.... ...O God, that I were a man! I would eat his heart in the market-place. .... men are only turned into tongue.... I cannot be a man with wishing; therefore I will die a woman with grieving.*	Beatrice cannot take physical action against a man, but the violence of her thoughts shows in her language. Claudio shamed Hero in public, and Beatrice would make him suffer in public as revenge. As a woman she cares more about emotions than public gestures, but that does not give her the physical power to kill.
Extract 2 Leonato seems more eager to blame Margaret than Claudio and the Prince.	*Leonato: ...Margaret was in some fault for this,....*	Leonato is always ready to believe the worst of a woman, even his own daughter, and Margaret is not only a woman, she is a servant.
Defeated in verbal battle, as usual, Benedick resorts to physical action.	*Benedick: Peace! I will stop your mouth. (Kissing her)*	Benedick and Beatrice finally join in a kiss: the battle between men and women is over.
Benedick's earlier attitudes make this all the more amusing for the audience.	*Benedick:... for man is a giddy thing,....*	The truth at last – man is just a changeable creature; it is women who are constant in love.
Every man needs a woman – Benedick, the scourge of women, now says so.	*Benedick: Prince, thou art sad: get thee a wife, get thee a wife!*	Benedick has come full circle in his attitude to women, and the audience love him for it.

Focus on language

Highlight the key words in the tables below and fill in the blank rows with your own points, quotations and personal responses.

Extract 1: Act 4, Scene 1, lines 196–325

Points	Quotations	Personal responses
The Friar's speech has several references to death. In his plan to restore Hero's reputation, Claudio has to believe she has died. Claudio has killed Hero's reputation through his accusation that she is not a virgin.	Friar: Your daughter here the princes left for dead or publish it that she is dead indeed or She dying or he shall hear she died upon his words or the supposition of the lady's death or Come, Lady, die to live	Throughout the speech the Friar makes it clear that Hero can only be saved by pretending that she is dead. By repeating this idea in several ways he is persuading Leonato to accept his plan.
Beatrice tries to persuade Benedick to kill Claudio by suggesting that he is not man enough to do it. The knowledge that she is helpless to do anything to help her cousin adds to her growing anger and her deep desire for revenge.	Beatrice: How much might the man deserve of me that would right her or It's a man's office, or O that I were a man or O God that I were a man or Manhood is melted into curtsies	Beatrice is challenging Benedick's masculinity by suggesting that he lacks the courage to avenge her cousin. The final insult she throws at him is that she, a mere woman, is more prepared to fight Claudio, than Benedick is. In her view, men are all talk and no action. Her attack on Benedick shows how frustrated she is that she cannot avenge Hero and is furious that someone who can do it, won't do it, hence her frequent and furious repetition of 'man'.
Hero's loss of her honour will have a devastating impact on her position in society. The Friar has made it clear that if his plan fails, Hero cannot return to her home as she will be vilified and shunned by the community. Her only option is to go to a nunnery and live her life in solitude, where she will be safe from the wagging tongues.	Beatrice: Infamy Friar: Out of all eyes, tongues, minds and injuries or Her wounded reputation	The image that is created of the fate that awaits Hero if her good name cannot be restored is an unpleasant one. She has been badly hurt by Claudio's accusation and she will suffer physical banishment as well as the emotional shock and pain that she has endured. The word 'wounded' illustrates just how serious the situation is for Hero.
Beatrice is enraged by what has happened to her dear cousin who she knows is innocent of the crime of being unfaithful to Claudio.	Beatrice: Slandered, scorned, dishonoured	The impact of these three words is very powerful – they all have negative meanings as they are harsh words which have overtones of injustice and cruelty.
The seriousness of Hero's situation is lightened for a moment when Benedick confesses his love for Beatrice.	Benedick: I love nothing in the world so well as you or By my sword Beatrice, thou lovest me.	The language of love that Benedick uses is linked to his profession as a soldier. By using the image of swearing by his sword he is staking his reputation as a soldier to show her just how serious he is about her.
This is a very tender moment in the play as the two characters who have previously fought each other, finally confess their true feelings	Benedick: I protest I love thee. Beatrice: I was about to protest I loved you.	The lovers echo one another's words, which unites them as they share not only the same words, but the same feelings too.
Benedick realises that if he wants to keep Beatrice's love he has to agree to her demand to 'Kill Claudio'.	Beatrice: Kill Claudio.	Beatrice's savagery here is more from the men's world of war than the woman's world of words – she wants a killing.

Focus on language

Mark brief quotations in your extracts using a different coloured highlighter for each of the themes shown below. Add your own quotations and annotations for these and for other themes you think are important.

Extract 2: Act 5, Scene 4

Points	Quotations	Personal responses
The dramatic tension in the play has hinged on mistaken identity. In this scene, when the truth is revealed, eyes and sight are mentioned several times to show that your eyes can sometimes deceive you.	Benedick: ...eye of favour or Benedick:....eye of love... or Claudio: Sweet, let me see your face.	Characters have been misled by what they think they have seen, as with Claudio and the Prince. Now, to make amends for that serious mistake, Claudio has agreed to marry someone he has never seen.
The battle of words between Beatrice and Benedick has blinded them to the fact that they love one another.	Leonato: That eye my daughter lent her. or The sight whereof I think you had from me,....	Benedick and Beatrice's mistrust of one another meant they could not see that they really loved one another. They needed other people to make them see it.
Hands and hearts are a recurring image in this scene. The hands symbolise the marriage ceremony when the couple are joined, which is how the play ends.	Claudio: ...written in his hand or Hero: Writ in my cousin's hand, ... or Benedick:.... our own hands against our hearts	The evidence that Benedick and Beatrice do love one another comes from the love poetry they wrote secretly about one another. Benedick knows he has won Beatrice's hand in marriage because she cannot deny what she has written about her love for him.
Claudio uses animal imagery to try and joke with Benedick. The banter is about sex and he thinks it will make Benedick lose his 'February face'.	Claudio: Savage bull or Noble beast in love Bull Jove had an amiable low	This crude joke is out of keeping at a wedding ceremony and shows that Claudio is as immature at the end of the play as he was at the beginning. Claudio does not realise that things have changed and that Benedick is still angry with him.
Benedick, who has not forgiven Claudio for what he did to Hero, twists the same image to insult Claudio.	Benedick: Some such strange bull leaped your father's cow and got a calf ... his bleat.	Benedick's sharp retort reveals that, unlike Claudio who he calls 'a calf', he has changed since the beginning of the play and the jokes that he once enjoyed now irritate him. Jokes about adultery and sex no longer amuse him because his love for Beatrice is pure and true. In order to be ready to marry Beatrice, Benedick has to become less of a man's man and more of a lover.
Benedick knew that he would be mocked for changing his mind over marriage, so turns his defence into attack, urging Don Pedro to marry.	Benedick: Dost thou think I care for a satire or an epigram? or Never flout at me for what I have said against it	Benedick is no longer the wit he was: he cares more about actions than about words.
Benedick's earlier comments about women were very critical, but he has changed.	Benedick: For man is a giddy thing, and this is my conclusion	The evidence of the play is that Benedick is right – men (who hold the power in the play) change their minds at least as much as women.
Now that Benedick has won Beatrice's hand in marriage, he is a happy man.	Benedick: Let's have a dance or our wives' or Get thee a wife, get thee a wife.	Benedick's happiness is evident here. He enjoys describing the women as 'our wives', and stresses the importance of marriage by advising the Prince to find himself a wife, just as he has done.

Focus on performance

Highlight the key words in the table below and fill in the blank rows with your own points, quotations and personal responses.

Extract 1: Act 4, Scene 1, lines 196–325

Points	Quotations	Personal responses
After the anger following the collapse of the marriage, the Friar needs to calm the situation.	Friar: *Pause awhile,* *And let my counsel sway you in this case.*	When the Friar says 'pause' and 'counsel' he should make calming gestures to the others on stage. When they hear the calm way he says these words the audience will sense a change in atmosphere. They will begin to feel that the Friar will solve the problem.
Leonato is so distressed and angry he is impatient with the Friar.	Leonato: *What shall become of this?* or Leonato: *What will this do?*	Leonato should ask these short questions impatiently as he can't see the point of the Friar's idea. The audience will see he won't be easily persuaded and they will be as puzzled as Leonato about the plan.
The Friar is calm in his arguing to try to persuade Leonato.	Friar: *... for so it falls out* and Friar: *So will it fare with Claudio.* and Friar: *... Then shall he mourn, ...*	Each sentence carefully builds the argument. The Friar should behave like a lawyer arguing a case in court. He should speak clearly and look at each of the others like a lawyer.
Benedick helps the Friar's argument.	Benedick: *... let the Friar advise you...* or Benedick: *... I will deal in this* *As secretly and justly...*	Benedick should move towards Leonato as he says these words, to emphasise his point. As Benedick joins in the argument, the audience will see that it is all the men who are sorting things out.
Beatrice is upset by what has happened to Hero.	Benedick: *Lady Beatrice, have you wept all this while?* or Beatrice: *Yea, and I will weep a while longer.*	Beatrice should be weeping and appear very upset. The audience will see the contrast with her normal behaviour and see how upset she is.
When they are alone, Benedick knows that Beatrice is upset and he has to talk to her carefully.	Benedick: *Is there any way to show such friendship?* or Benedick: *... I do believe your fair cousin is wronged.*	He asks her questions politely and says he believes her. He should speak gently to show he sympathises with her. The audience will see from his behaviour that he is being much kinder to her now.
Beatrice is thrown into confusion when he declares his love.	Beatrice: *... I confess nothing, nor I deny nothing.* or Beatrice: *... believe me not, and yet I lie not:...*	Beatrice's short sentences and contradictions show she is surprised and not sure how to answer. She should behave in a flustered way and speak hurriedly, showing that she is changing her mind. This makes the audience realise how she has been affected by his words.
Beatrice's behaviour changes when she asks him to commit murder.	Beatrice: *Kill Claudio.* or Beatrice: *There is no love in you.*	Beatrice should say these lines sharply to make a contrast with the gentler speeches before. She has persuaded him to promise her anything, then suddenly changes as she demands he kill Claudio.
Beatrice tries to leave and Benedick tries to stop her.	Benedick: *Tarry, sweet Beatrice.* and Beatrice: *... I pray you, let me go.*	They should struggle with each other and Benedick pleads while she replies coldly. Benedick's begging shows the audience how much he has changed since the start of the play now that he is in love with her.
Beatrice's fierce anger contrasts with his pleading tone.	Beatrice: *O that I were a man!* and Benedick: *Hear me, Beatrice –*	Beatrice's anger is shown in long speeches full of repetition with angry gestures and contrasts with him begging her. The audience see that Benedick is still trying to show some loyalty for Claudio, while Beatrice hates him.

Focus on performance

Highlight the key words in the table below and fill in the blank rows with your own points, quotations and personal responses.

Extract 2: Act 5, Scene 4

Points	Quotations	Personal responses
The Friar and the others are relieved.	Friar: *Did I not tell you she was innocent?* **or** Antonio: *Well, I am glad that all things sort so well.*	The characters should speak their lines in a tone of relief and they should look happy. This is a contrast with the first extract when everyone was angry and concerned.
Benedick asks to marry Beatrice.	Benedick: *… my will is your good will….* **or** Benedick: *Your niece regards me with an eye of favour*	He must behave and speak politely to persuade Leonato. His polite speech and behaviour show the audience how much he wants to marry Beatrice.
Benedick no longer wants to joke with Claudio.	Benedick: *… some such strange bull leaped your father's cow….* **or** Benedick: *… you have just his bleat.*	Benedick should make this bitter comment harshly and not be joking. His changed behaviour to Claudio shows he has become more mature and the audience will notice the contrast with his earlier behaviour.
There is a clear contrast on the stage between the men and the women.	Claudio: *Which is the lady I must seize upon?* **or** Claudio: *… she's mine. …*	The women come in politely, wearing masks, while the men inspect and discuss them. This makes the marriage seem like a market controlled by men.
Claudio and Don Pedro are amazed to see Hero.	Claudio: *Another Hero!* **or** Don Pedro: *Hero that is dead!*	They should speak in a surprised tone which will make the audience sense the happiness and contrast with the anger of the first extract.
Beatrice and Benedick start to behave as they did before.	Benedick: *They swore that you were almost sick for me.* **and** Beatrice: *They swore that you were well-nigh dead for me.*	They go back to their verbal games, each trying to outdo the other, but now the audience realise they are only pretending to be distant with one another and will soon marry.
Benedick stops the argument by kissing her and then talks of his happiness.	Benedick: *Peace! I will stop your mouth.* **or** Benedick: *A college of wit-crackers cannot flout me out of my humour.*	Benedick should suddenly grab her for the kiss. The physical action of kissing her finally stops their battle and then his happiness is clear. The kiss is the sign the audience have been waiting for.
There is a final dance with all the characters joining in.	Benedick: *Let's have a dance….* **or** Benedick: *… play, music.*	All the characters should begin to dance with joy, showing the audience their relief that everything has worked out.
The messenger interrupts the dance.	Messenger: *… your brother John is ta'en in flight,….* **or** Benedick: *I'll devise thee brave punishments for him.*	The dance should stop as he comes in with the news and then restart even more joyfully after Benedick promises that Don John will be punished.

The Key Stage 3 Shakespeare test

How to approach the test

Remember that:

- The Shakespeare test accounts for 18 out of the 50 marks for reading. You gain marks by showing you understand and have responded to Shakespeare.
- The way you write matters because it enables you to make your points effectively, but you will not be judged on how well you write. No marks are given (or taken off) for spelling or expression.
- The extracts you will have to write about will be printed in the test paper. Don't make the mistake of writing about all of the set scenes – concentrate on those two extracts.
- PQR (**P**oint, **Q**uotation, **R**esponse) is better than PEE (**P**oint, **E**xplanation, **E**xample) because it includes your personal reaction to the play.
- Short quotations are better than long ones because they save you time in the test.

Top tips for the test

- Keep in mind performances of the play that you have seen, in the theatre or on video.
- Remember what it was like acting out the set scenes with other people.
- Make sure that you are familiar with the layout and style of questions by looking at tests from previous years.
- Read the question aloud in your head two or three times until you realise what it is really asking you to do.
- Don't ever just tell the story – answer the question.
- Time spent on planning is time well spent. Practise doing a plan in five minutes so that in the real test you can create a plan quickly and effectively.
- Plan so that your main points are in a sensible order that responds to the question.
- Provide evidence in quotation or refer to what happens and is said to support your points. (Don't waste time copying out long quotations.)
- Make sure that your conclusion relates back to the question.
- Leave time (but not too much) at the end of the test to read through what you have written.

What will the questions be on?

The question on *Much Ado About Nothing* should be on **one** of the areas (or 'big ideas') below, although you usually need to refer to the other areas as part of your answer.

- Why **characters** behave as they do in the extracts given.
- The impact of the **language** used in the extracts.
- **Ideas, themes** and **issues** that are relevant to the extracts.
- How these extracts might be **performed** in the theatre.

Key Stage 3 marking

How will my answer be marked?

The emphasis in marking will depend on the focus of the question, but generally answers are awarded level 5 or above if they:

- include comment on both of the extracts given on the paper
- reveal some understanding of character and dramatic action
- refer to the main features of the language in the extracts and the effect this language might have
- show some awareness of how an audience might respond
- illustrate points made, by picking out words or phrases from the text as evidence
- include your personal response to specific aspects of the extracts.

Answers on Shakespeare are allocated to mark bands. The characteristics of different mark bands for a question on **language** are set out below.

	General characteristics	What will that look like to an examiner?
1	A few simple facts and opinions about the focus of the question. Some re-telling and answers only partly relevant.	Comments are general and show limited understanding of the extracts or the question, e.g. *The Friar talks too much.* The two extracts are not treated equally, and there may be much storytelling with big chunks of quotation used without explanation.
2	Some awareness of the more obvious aspects of the question. Some broad references to the way characters speak or behave.	Some comment on what characters do and say. The two extracts may not be treated equally and simple references may not be linked with comments. Little comment on the effect of characters' use of language, although there may be reference to some words or phrases, e.g *The Friar uses long words which shows he is educated and not as upset as the family.*
3	Shows general understanding of characters' feelings and of the way language reveals character and refers to textual evidence.	Secure general understanding of the impression an audience might have of characters and what their language shows about how they develop. Points are generally illustrated by relevant references to the text, although comments may be repeated rather than developed. Limited comment on the effects of language, e.g. *The Friar's language is balanced and calm, because he is the one thinking what to do.*
4	Shows awareness of characters' feelings and how this is shown through language and its effects. References show consciousness of how Shakespeare wants his characters to speak.	May provide some discussion of the impressions an audience might get of a character from the way they speak or behave. Relevant references from both extracts will be included and there should be clear understanding of the broader context of the play. Explicit, if limited, comment on the effects of a character's use of language would be expected, e.g. *The Friar's calm language 'maintain a mourning ostentation' contrasts with emotional Leonato.*
5	Clear focus on the question asked, with understanding of the way language is used and of its effects. Well-chosen references to the text justify comments as part of an overall argument.	A relevant and focused answer which engages confidently with both extracts. Aspects of the text will be explored, not just explained, in ways that show a wider understanding of the play's development. The selection of well-chosen references builds into a sustained argument which includes comment on the dramatic effect of the language used, e.g. *The Friar's calm and balanced language 'maintain a mourning ostentation' gives him the audience's attention and contrasts with the helpless emotion of Leonato.*
6	Coherent analysis of characters' actions and attitudes. Appreciation of the features and effects of language. Comments and precisely selected references to the text are integrated into well-developed argument.	A focused and developed analysis of the impression created by a character through language and action on stage. The answer engages analytically with both extracts, showing insight into the less obvious aspects of the text and an ability to contextualise ideas. Appreciation of the features and effects of language is well supported by integrated references. There may be recognition of the possibility of different interpretations of the text, e.g. *This is a moment of near-tragedy, but the Friar's calm and balanced language 'maintain a mourning ostentation' changes the mood, gives him the audience's attention (in contrast to the distracted emotion of Leonato) and points to a positive outcome. After all, this is a comedy.*

Sample questions

Thinking about the question: an example

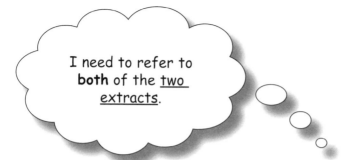

I need to refer to **both** of the <u>two extracts</u>.

<u>Show</u> means I must write about how the audience react to what is said and what happens on stage.

What do these <u>two</u> extracts <u>show</u> about <u>attitudes</u> to <u>love and marriage?</u>

<u>Attitudes</u> are revealed through what characters do and (especially) what they say.

Love and marriage are key themes of the play – I need to explain how are they presented in these extracts.

Sample questions

Themes
- Deception
- Honour and revenge
- Love and marriage
- Male and female

- What do these two extracts show about attitudes to love and marriage?
- What idea of honour might an audience gain from these two extracts?
- Explain what part deception plays in these two extracts.
- What do these two extracts show about relationships between men and women?

Character
- Explain how these two extracts reveal changes in the feelings that Beatrice and Benedick have for each other.
- What differences might an audience notice between Benedick's behaviour and attitudes in extract 1 and extract 2?

Language
- How does the language used in these two extracts show the changes in the relationship between Beatrice and Benedick?
- How does the language used in these two extracts show that characters respond differently to Claudio's treatment of Hero?

Performance
- What advice might the director of a school performance give to the actors playing Beatrice and Benedick on how to respond to each other in these two extracts?
- If you were the actor playing Beatrice, how would you show the range of her feelings in these two extracts?

Sample answer with examiner's comments

If you were an actor playing Beatrice, how would you show the range of emotions in these two extracts?

In extract one I would show the audience that Beatrice is upset by Hero's public shame. I would sit in a crumpled heap on the stage and look miserable. Suddenly I would show how angry I am by saying something completely out of character; asking for a man to 'right her!' When Benedick blurts out that he loves Beatrice, I would stand up in total confusion and show this by saying 'nothing' three times, as if in a muddle. One minute I would look at Benedick and say' I loved nothing so well as you', then turn away saying 'believe me not' then turn back to say 'I lie not'. Finally, in confusion, I would burst into tears and speak in a pathetic tone: 'I am sorry for my cousin'.

Benedick should give me his handkerchief and I would blow my nose very noisily, but still show suspicion of him by saying 'Will you not eat your word.' When Benedick asks what he can do for her I would shock the audience and Benedick by pausing, then changing my tone from love to hate.

'Kill Claudio.'

When he refuses I would turn angrily away from him and coldly say 'You kill me', putting strong emphasis on 'me' to make Benedick feel guilty. I would make Beatrice talk like a man defending the honour of her family. It should be serious and yet funny because she is talking about the honour she made fun of at the start of the play.

She uses a male style of speaking so I would say 'slandered, scorned, dishonoured' very slowly, with each word more dramatic than the last as if I were winding myself up until I shout out with frustration:

'O God that I were a man!'

This is so unlike Beatrice the man-hater that the audience would laugh even though she is so serious and so violent.

'I would eat his heart in the market place'

I would become more and more angry as I mock Claudio, spitting out 'Count Comfect'. I believe that Beatrice is taking advantage of Benedick's love because she suggests he should challenge Claudio for her love. So I would finally be very melodramatic

---

Comment boxes (examiner's comments):

In a performance essay you must link **how** an actor would speak with **why** he would speak or act like that. Link action to meaning and context, e.g. Beatrice says 'Kill Claudio.' Her sad tone should change to anger as she thinks how Claudio has publicly shamed her cousin

Comment on change of tone and why it happens to show a change of emotions

Clear focus on why Beatrice is so angry with Claudio and how she shows her emotions

Clear focus on how Beatrice's language would show her anger for Claudio and the effect she has on Benedick

Discussion about the effects of language and why Beatrice should speak as she does

Sample answer with examiner's comments (continued)

with my hand on my brow when I say I will die 'with grieving'. I feel that Beatrice has won her battle to enlist Benedick's support.

Discussion about what has happened to make Beatrice calm down. Hero's innocence has been proved

In the second extract Beatrice has calmed down now that Hero has been proved innocent. Now Beatrice should return to her normal way of behaving with Benedick as if the past scene never happened. Benedick is still very serious because he has asked Leonato for her hand but Beatrice does not know this. I would speak in a casual joking tone when replying to Benedick.

'Do you not love me?'

'Why no, no more than reason.'

Awareness of the effects of language to show the difference between the emotional language of extract 1 and the return to the word games that Beatrice and Benedick played before Hero's disgrace

It is only after Claudio and Hero produce their writings about their love for each other that Benedick realises her game and says he will have her because he pities her. Beatrice should not give up easily and I would make her try to save face by saying she will have him 'to save your life'. However when she uses the word 'yield' she should sigh as if she seems unwilling to give up her 'merry war'. Benedick kisses her to 'stop her mouth'. From this point on Beatrice does not speak again. I would go to Hero and stand with her whilst Benedick has the last words with the men.

Clear focus on the casual language of Beatrice, who tries to disguise her love as concern for Benedick's life

Discussion about how Beatrice does not want to admit her love and how she wants to cover up her feelings because she still doubts Benedick

Overall I would want to show that Beatrice has the same passions and feelings as a man, but when she wants something done she will play the grieving woman to get it.

There is clear commentary on the range of Beatrice's emotions and how the actor could show these in performance. The change in her emotions is shown. Some points are developed, especially in extract 1. Relevant references are used to illustrate these changes by showing how performance would convey the effects of language.

Planning a character answer

Spend at least five minutes on planning in the test.

> **Explain how these two extracts reveal changes in the feelings that Beatrice and Benedick have for each other.**

Read and re-read the question **very** carefully, and underline or highlight the key words such as <u>changes</u> and <u>feelings</u>.

The focus is on **how** changes in characters' feelings are shown and **why** the relationship between Beatrice and Benedick develops as it does.

I must mention both extracts, and keep in mind that these characters are in a performance on a stage like The Globe, not just in a book.

My key points will be:
- By extract 1 Beatrice and Benedick are no longer enemies – they share concern for Hero and for justice.
- Once Hero's innocence is known, they resume their *war of wit* in extract 2 until (as the audience knew they would) they mockingly declare their mutual love.

I must have a powerful opening point and an effective way of ending. My quotations or references need to be very brief.

My comments on words will include:
- Their uncertainties show because their expressions of love often include negative words – *I do love <u>nothing</u> in this world so well as you*
- Benedick's genuine concern for Beatrice shows in words: *have you wept all this while?...I am engaged.*
- We laugh when Beatrice finally yields upon great persuasion, whilst Benedick's readiness to endure mockery is evidence of his love – *man is a giddy thing.*

Language is very important. I must say **how** and **why** the effect of particular words is important in revealing character.

My comments on what happens on stage will include:
- their shared concern over Hero's disgrace
- Beatrice and Benedick's reactions on finding out that they have been fooled about each other's feelings
- Benedick silencing Beatrice at last with a loving kiss is a powerful image on stage. Having been apart throughout the play, they finish physically together.

I will comment on **why** these events reveal **how** their relationship changes.

My conclusion would:
Refer back to the title with comments on how the shared emotions of extract 1 prepare us for the declarations of affection in extract 2, whilst the language (*but no more than reason*) reminds us of their early wordfights.

Have I kept the focus throughout on evidence for changes in feelings?

Planning a theme answer

Spend at least five minutes on planning in the test.

Explain what part deception plays in these two extracts.

Read and re-read the question **very** carefully, and underline or highlight the key words such as *deception*.

The focus is on **deception** and therefore about the part deceiving people plays in the near-tragic Hero/Claudio relationship and the comic Beatrice/Benedick relationship.

I must mention **both** extracts, and keep in mind that this is a performance on a stage like The Globe, not just a book to be read.

My key points will be:
- There are different types of deception.
- The truth about Hero is revealed through deception.
- The 'true' love of Beatrice and Benedick is created through deception.

I must have a powerful opening point and an effective way of ending, and must keep quotations or references very brief.

My comments on words will include:
- Friar: ... *die to live*
- Claudio: *Sweet, let me see your face*
- Benedick:...*your uncle and the Prince and Claudio have been deceived. They swore you did.* (and Beatrice's parallel reply)

Language is very important. I must say **how** and **why** the effect of particular words is significant.

My comments on what happens on stage will include:
- the plan to pretend Hero is dead
- Claudio marrying an unseen bride
- Beatrice and Benedick finding out they have been fooled about each other's feelings.

I will comment on **why** and **how** these events could be presented to emphasise this theme of deception.

I will say **why** these events matter and **how** the audience might think that deception can be both good and evil.

My conclusion would:
Refer back to the title with comments on how deception has been the key to bringing sorrow and eventually joy to the main characters in both 'plots', which could make an audience reflect that the theatre itself uses deception to show us truths about the world and about ourselves.

Have I kept the focus on deception?

Planning a language answer

Spend at least five minutes on planning in the test.

How does the language used in these two extracts show that characters respond differently to Claudio's treatment of Hero?

Read and re-read the question **very** carefully, and underline or highlight the key words such as *language, two extracts, respond differently to Claudio's treatment*.

I must mention **both** extracts, and keep in mind that this is a performance on a stage like The Globe, not just a book to be read.

The focus is on **how** the language used reveals characters' response to Claudio's treatment of Hero.

My key points will be:
- Language is the most important guide to differences in what characters are feeling.
- The language in the two extracts is significantly different.

I must have a powerful opening point and an effective way of ending, and must keep quotations or references very brief.

I will explore these points by referring to:
- The Friar knows that Claudio is not all bad and will be devastated to hear of Hero's death – *then shall he mourn* and *wish he had not accused her*
- Benedick knows Claudio is to blame for what has happened to Hero – *fair cousin is wronged*
- *Kill Claudio* in extract 1, which shows the degree of Beatrice's passionate resentment of Claudio and her desire to see him die for what he has done to Hero
- Leonato calls Claudio *Young Claudio* in extract 2, which shows he has some affection for him
- Hero calls herself *your other wife* in extract 2, which shows she has forgiven him for what he did to her.

Language is very important. I must explain the dramatic effect of particular words.

However, I will also point out that:
- Benedick is not totally forgiving (*February face* and the insulting *bleat*) although he ends *Come, come, we are friends*
- *Benedick the married man* means that Claudio's conduct has not undermined the idea of marriage
- Benedick makes an effort to make his peace with Claudio by saying *Come, come, we are friends* because he knows they are now part of the same family.

I must say **why** and **how** language reveals characters' feelings here.

My conclusion would:
Refer to the title with comments on the intended effect of language. In extract 1 the language is serious and describes the pain and suffering Claudio has caused to the family. This contrasts with happier language in extract 2 which talks about love and marriage and a new start. This shows that the other characters have forgiven Claudio's treatment of Hero now that he accepts that he has slandered her and is willing to marry her cousin as penance for his mistake.

Have I kept the title in mind throughout?

Planning a performance answer

Spend at least 5 minutes on planning in the test.

What advice might the director of a school performance give to the actors playing Beatrice and Benedick on how to respond to each other in these two extracts?

Read and re-read the question **very** carefully, and underline or highlight the key words such as *Beatrice and Benedick* and *respond to each other*.

The focus is on **why** those playing Beatrice and Benedick should speak and act on stage in particular ways to help the audience understand their feelings.

I must mention **both** extracts, and keep in mind that this is a performance on a stage like The Globe, not just a book to be read.

My key points will be how to show:
- reactions to Hero's humiliation
- attitudes to each other
- changes in mood during the extracts
- how their performance compares in the two extracts.

I must have a powerful opening point and an effective way of ending, and must keep quotations or references very brief.

My advice on how to say words will include:
- the 'merry war' of words in both extracts
- Why a different tone is needed for *Kill Claudio* and *I am engaged* in extract 1
- *No more than reason* and *I will stop your mouth* in extract 2.

Language is very important. I must say **how** to speak particular words and explain **why** their effect is significant.

My advice on how to act on stage will be:
How to show the relationship through facial expressions, gestures, position on stage and movement (I needn't bother about costumes or props).

I would comment on **why** and **how** Benedick looks at Beatrice, his movements and his kiss.

I must say **why** and **how** Beatrice should show her anger and grief on stage and the ways she looks at Benedick with laughter and with love.

My conclusion would:
Refer to the title with comments on the intended effect of language and give a sense of how the audience might respond to Benedick and Beatrice because of the actions and gestures I have suggested.

Have I kept the title in mind throughout?